Save and Grow

Ricardo Moreno

Copyright Page

First edition

Index

Why Saving Doesn't Mean Sacrificing Your Life

Many people believe that saving means living with constant sacrifices, giving up things they like, such as going out to dinner, traveling, or even buying something small that makes them happy. This idea has created a misconception of what saving really means, and it is precisely this mentality that can make you feel unmotivated or stressed when you think about your finances. But what if I told you that saving does not have to be a sentence of deprivation, but rather a path to a fuller, freer, and calmer life?

The key is to understand that saving is not the same as restricting everything that gives you pleasure. Saving is learning to manage your money wisely, so that you can enjoy what you love without constantly worrying about the future. Imagine that you have a budget that allows you to enjoy your hobbies and fun times, but at the same time, you are saving for your most important goals, such as having an emergency fund or making an investment that allows you to grow financially. You don't have to choose between one thing or the other; it's about finding the balance.

For example, maybe you love going out to dinner with friends on the weekends, but you'd also like to have savings for a trip you've been dreaming about for years. Instead of stopping dining out altogether, you can make conscious choices, like choosing more affordable restaurants or limiting the number of outings to a few times a month. This allows you to continue enjoying those moments, while still keeping your long-term goals in mind. It's not about giving up, it's about prioritizing smartly.

What many people overlook is that by learning to manage your money effectively, saving with purpose, you are actually creating greater freedom. By having consistent, planned savings, you feel more secure and less anxious. You have the peace of mind of knowing that if an emergency arises, you have a financial cushion. This is true power. You no longer feel like money controls you; you control money.

Plus, saving doesn't mean making huge sacrifices all the time. Sometimes, small adjustments are enough, like stopping unnecessary purchases, avoiding impulse buys, or reviewing your monthly subscriptions to see if you're really getting the most out of them. If you take control of those details, you'll see how your ability to save increases without the need for big sacrifices. Those small changes, added up over time, can have a big impact on your financial well-being.

Another important aspect is that saving gives you the freedom to enjoy life in the long term without worry. When you don't have debts weighing you down, when you've built up an emergency fund, or when you've invested in your future, you can relax more in the present. Saving doesn't mean you have to live a strict life, but it's about making smart choices and not letting your finances be a burden in your daily life.

Instead of thinking of saving as a kind of deprivation, see it as a form of empowerment. You're taking control of your finances and ensuring that you can live a peaceful life, enjoying the present while also being prepared for the future. It's not about giving up the things you enjoy, but rather being more conscious of your choices so that you can continue to enjoy them guilt-free and with greater freedom.

The good thing about saving is that you don't have to do it all at once or in a drastic way. It's a gradual process. Start with small goals, like saving a percentage of your salary each month. Then, as you get used to saving, you can set bigger goals, like creating an emergency fund or starting to invest. But it all starts with the initial step of changing your mindset and understanding that you don't have to sacrifice your life for a better future, but that you can have both, now and later, if you know how to manage your finances.

In short, saving doesn't mean living frugally or depriving yourself of what brings you joy. It means making smart choices, setting priorities, and finding a balance between enjoying the present and preparing for the future. Saving is a tool that allows you to live with less stress, more control, and greater confidence in your financial life. By shifting your focus to saving, you give yourself the power to enjoy a fuller life, knowing that every decision you make brings you closer to your goals and dreams.

The Power of Conscious Budgeting

Conscious budgeting isn't simply a list of numbers or a set of categories on a spreadsheet. It's not just about writing down what you spend and what you save. The true power of conscious budgeting lies in how it connects you to your priorities, allows you to make informed decisions about your money, and helps you live according to what really matters to you. Instead of seeing budgeting as a constraint or a boring chore, imagine it as your treasure map — a tool that guides you to reach your financial goals without sacrificing what you truly enjoy.

The first thing you need to understand is that a conscious budget is more than just keeping track of what comes in and what goes out. It's an active process of reflecting on your values and priorities. Before you start jotting down any numbers, you need to pause and think about what you really want to achieve. Do you want to travel more? Save for your children's education? Or maybe you'd rather reduce your debts and live more peacefully? Defining your goals will allow you to give your budget a real purpose. It's not just about saving money, but saving with a clear purpose that motivates you and keeps you focused.

Once you have your goals in mind, it's time to start consciously dividing up your money. The key is to allocate your resources in ways that get you closer to those goals, without neglecting what's important to you right now. This means being honest with yourself about what you're willing to spend. A conscious budget doesn't tell you "don't spend on that," but instead invites you to reflect: Is this what I really want to do with my money right now? Maybe you want that expensive coffee every morning, but if your goal is to save up for a vacation, then it's a matter of prioritizing what gets you closer to that goal.

The next step is to track your spending. But instead of just jotting it down on a spreadsheet, do it with intention. Ask yourself why you spend on each thing. Is it a necessity? Or is it something you've been buying out of habit or because it's something "everyone does"? This reflection will help you see where you can make adjustments without feeling like you're sacrificing what really matters to you. It's not about aggressively cutting your spending, but rather finding ways to spend your money more consciously. Maybe you don't need to buy new clothes every month or subscribe to every streaming service. But if you realize that those expenses aren't getting you closer to your goals, you can make adjustments without losing what you truly value.

A conscious budget also encourages you to think about the future. It's easy to focus on immediate needs, but the real power of a budget is in planning for the long term. If you're not putting some of your money toward savings or investing, you may feel stuck in an endless cycle of living paycheck to paycheck. But with a conscious budget, you can start saving regularly, even if it's just small amounts at first. The important thing is to create a habit. This habit will allow you to build an emergency fund, save for big goals like buying a home or retirement, and feel more financially secure. Even if you can only save a small amount at first, the key is to get started. The power is in consistency.

It's equally important to recognize that a conscious budget gives you flexibility. Unlike a traditional budget, which can feel rigid and restrictive, a conscious budget allows you to be flexible based on life's circumstances. If one month you spend a little more on a personal project or celebration, that's okay. The important thing is that you know why you did it and how that fits into your bigger picture. If your budget allows for these small deviations without compromising your goals, it's a sign that you're managing your money in a healthy way. Conscious budgeting isn't a hard-and-fast rule, but rather a tool to make your decisions more intentional.

Plus, as you spend more time working on your conscious budget, you'll notice your relationship with money starting to change. You'll no longer see your finances as a burden or as something that's slipping through your fingers. You'll see money as a tool to create the life you want. A conscious budget helps you become more aware of how you spend, save, and invest, allowing you to make more informed decisions that are aligned with your values. Not only does this improve your financial well-being, but it also gives you a greater sense of control and empowerment.

Ultimately, the power of a conscious budget lies in its ability to transform your approach to money. It allows you to see beyond numbers and restrictions, and helps you make choices that bring you closer to what you really want in life. It's not just about making your money work, it's about making sure every expense and every saving is in line with your desires and dreams. By being more conscious of how you manage your money, you can live more freely, more aligned with what really matters to you, and more confident that you're taking control of your future.

Ant Expenses and How to Eradicate Them Effortlessly

Small expenses are those little expenses that usually don't seem important at the time, but over time, they add up and can become a big drag on your finances. Often, we don't even notice them. They're the morning coffees, impulse purchases, snacks, or those subscriptions we automatically renew without thinking about it. These expenses are invisible, but dangerous, and if you're not careful, they can consume a significant portion of your money without you even realizing it.

The most frustrating thing about small expenses is that they don't feel like a real expense. For example, you spend $3 or $5 on a coffee in the morning and it seems insignificant. Then you buy a small bottle of water, then a snack at the store, and it all seems so small that you don't even register it as a major expense. But if you add up all of those small expenses over the month, you'll be surprised at how much money you've been mindlessly wasting. A coffee every day can cost you over $100 a month, just for taking a small step to the coffee shop each morning. And if that's not enough, often these small expenses are just the tip of the iceberg, because they're combined with other small expenses that don't seem urgent either, but together, they create a hole in your budget.

Eliminating small spending doesn't require a lifestyle revolution or a great deal of discipline, but it does require some awareness and some simple adjustments. The first thing you need to do is start recognizing them. Simply being aware that these expenses exist is the first step toward taking control of your money. Take a few days to observe what you're mindlessly spending on. Do this without putting too much pressure on yourself, just as an exercise in awareness. You might be surprised to realize how many of these small expenses are adding up without you even realizing it.

Once you've identified them, the next step is to start making small, easy-to-implement changes. It's not about cutting out all your little indulgences at once, but rather finding ways to make them more conscious. For example, if you're a fan of morning coffee, instead of going to the same store every day to buy one, how about making it at home? You can invest in a good coffee machine or a reusable to-go cup, and make your favorite drink for a fraction of the price. It’s a small change, but every time you make it, you’re avoiding an unnecessary expense that adds up over time.

Another common expense is subscriptions. We often subscribe to streaming services, apps, or magazines, and forget to cancel them when we're done using them. Take a look at your recurring subscriptions. Are you really using all of those services? If you have Netflix, Amazon Prime, Spotify, and other services, are you getting the most out of them? If you don't use them often, cancel the ones you don't need. A small adjustment here can save you a lot of money in the long run without you having to sacrifice much.

Plus, technology is full of micro-spending that can slip through our fingers. If you're someone who buys apps, games, or in-app products, you may not even realize how much you're spending each month. Review your purchase history on your phone and in your app accounts. Make a list of these expenses and decide if they're really necessary. You can eliminate unnecessary purchases and limit impulse purchases. This doesn't mean you have to give up on enjoying an app or game, but it's important to keep track of these small expenses.

A simple and effective strategy to control small spending is to set a monthly limit. Dedicate a small percentage of your budget to these personal pleasures, but make sure that they do not become an excessive expense. If you decide that you have $50 a month to spend on these small pleasures, make sure that you do not exceed that amount. This will give you a clearer control of how much you are spending and will prevent those expenses from getting out of control.

Another way to eradicate small spending is to keep track of your finances. There are several apps and online tools that allow you to monitor your expenses and see what you are spending your money on. These tools can be very helpful in keeping a clear and accurate record of your small expenses. Whenever you notice that you are spending on something unnecessary, you can immediately adjust it, allowing you to keep a closer control over your finances.

Finally, it is important to remember that eliminating small expenses does not mean living a life without pleasure. It is not about eliminating all small expenses, but rather being more aware of them. The idea is that you can continue to enjoy those small things, but without them becoming a burden on your budget. If you take the time to reflect on what really brings you happiness and what is just an automatic and meaningless expense, it will be easier for you to decide what to eliminate or reduce.

In short, eliminating small expenses doesn't require huge sacrifices. It's about being aware of those small, invisible expenses and making simple adjustments in your daily life. By identifying and controlling these expenses, you can free up a significant amount of money that you can allocate to your real financial goals. These small changes will not only improve your financial well-being, but they will also help you live more consciously and with greater control over your money.

The Habit That Transforms You

There is one habit that, when adopted, has the power to transform not only your financial life, but many other areas of your life as well. That habit is consistency. The reason this habit is so powerful is because it is not about making big changes all at once, but about small adjustments that stick over time. The key is daily repetition, making conscious choices every day that bring you closer to your goal, no matter how small the step may seem.

Imagine you want to start saving, but you don't know where to start. Many people get discouraged because they think they need to save large amounts of money right away, or that they need to make a radical change in their lifestyle. The reality is that you don't need to make huge sacrifices to get started. You just need to start with what you can. At first it may not seem like enough, but the magic of consistency is that every little step counts. If you save a small amount every day, say, five or ten dollars, those small savings will add up over time and create a solid foundation. Those five or ten dollars may seem insignificant at first, but if you save them consistently, you'll have accumulated a significant amount by the end of the month, and then the year.

The problem with many people trying to save is that they focus on immediate results. They want to see large amounts of money in their bank account quickly, but they forget that longer-lasting changes take time. Consistency is the trick to making those small habits add up to something big. When you focus on being consistent, you realize that it's not about the amount of money you save, but the discipline of saving every day. This habit of saving, even a small amount, has a much bigger impact than making a big effort a couple of times a year.

This habit of consistency also has a cumulative effect. If, for example, you commit to saving 10% of your income each month, even though it may seem like a small percentage at first, over time you will notice how your savings add up. The key is to do it month after month, without exceptions. By the end of the year, you will have saved a significant amount, but more importantly, you will have created a habit that will continue to grow. It's like going to the gym: the first few days may be tough, but if you're consistent, the results start to show.

Consistency is also important when it comes to investing. Many people think they need to have a large amount of money to start investing, but that's not true. You can start investing with small amounts and do it consistently. If you are consistent in investing, no matter how small the amounts, over time you will see how that money multiplies thanks to compound interest. It doesn't matter if you can only invest $50 or $100 a month at first, the important thing is to do it consistently. The key is to let time and repetition work in your favor.

Another important aspect of consistency is that it allows you to create an abundance mindset. Often, people who struggle financially focus on what they lack. They focus on what they don't have and the difficulties they face. But, when you focus on the habit of consistency, you start to focus on what you can control. By making daily choices and being consistent, you start to realize that you are on the path to success, even if the results aren't immediate. This gives you a sense of control and motivates you to keep going.

This habit of consistency extends to other areas of life as well. If you apply it to your finances, you'll find that you can apply the same principle to other goals you've set for yourself. The key is to not give up when the results aren't immediate, but to stick with the process. For example, if your goal is to lose weight, you can apply the same principle: small habits, like eating healthier or exercising every day, will get you there over time. Consistency helps you build a lifestyle that allows you to move toward your goals effectively.

Plus, consistency helps you create habits that become naturally integrated into your life. At first, you may have to make a conscious effort to save or invest. But over time, those habits become automatic. You no longer have to think about it all the time. You start making these changes so naturally that you don't even notice it, and that's what really makes a difference. Consistent habits become a part of your daily life, allowing you to focus on other important areas of your life without constantly worrying about money.

Finally, the power of consistency isn’t just about finances. It also affects how you feel about yourself. By being consistent, you prove to yourself that you are capable of achieving what you set out to do. This sense of self-efficacy is critical to keeping going. Every time you stick to your habit of saving, investing, or doing something for your financial well-being, you feel more empowered and confident in your abilities. This confidence carries over into other aspects of your life, and gives you the motivation to keep improving in each area.

In short, the habit that transforms you is consistency. It's not about making big changes right away or expecting quick results. It's about taking small steps every day, no matter how insignificant they may seem. By being consistent, you'll be building a more secure future and achieving your goals effortlessly. The key is to keep going, no matter the ups and downs, and remember that progress is a gradual process. When consistency becomes part of your daily life, you realize that transformation is not in the great effort, but in the constant discipline that leads you to success.

Define your Financial Goals and Prioritize Them

Defining your financial goals is one of the most important steps you can take on your path to financial stability. If you don't know where you're going, it's very difficult to know how to get there. Goals give you clear direction and motivate you to keep going, even when the challenges seem overwhelming. Without clear goals, your money is scattered across small expenses, and there's no way to measure progress. That's why the first step in any financial plan should be to precisely define what you want to achieve. Not only does this help you organize your finances, but it also gives you the motivation to make the necessary sacrifices and make the right decisions.

The first thing you need to do is think about what you really want to achieve. It may sound simple, but many people feel lost because they don't have a clear vision of their goals. What would you like to do with your money? Maybe you want to buy a house, travel, start a business, or save for your children's education. It's important to take the time to reflect on your desires, not just in terms of what sounds good, but what really matters to you. Sometimes people feel pressured by what others consider a "good goal," like owning a home, without asking themselves if that's really what they want. Take the time to figure out what's important to you. If your goals don't resonate with you, it will be much harder to stay focused on them.

Once you're clear on what you want to achieve, it's time to put those goals on paper. Write them down. When you write down your goals, you commit to them in a more tangible way. It's like you make them more real. But don't just make them vague, like "I want to save money." Be specific about how much money you need to save and in what time frame. For example, "I want to save $10,000 in the next 12 months for my emergency fund." The clearer and more specific you are, the easier it will be to stay on track. A vague goal doesn't have the same power as a well-defined one. And the same goes for any financial goal you have: buying a home, paying off debt, or investing for retirement. Be specific about the amount, time frame, and reason for your goal.

Once you've defined your goals, the next step is to prioritize them. Life isn't always linear, and unexpected situations often arise that can make some goals more urgent than others. But the order in which you work on your goals is critical to not feeling overwhelmed or lost. Not all goals are equally urgent or important at the moment. You need to evaluate what's most critical to you and when is the right time to do it.

For example, if you have high-interest credit card debt, that goal should probably be your number one priority. Debt, especially high-interest debt, can eat away at your money quickly, and if you don't pay it off, it will hold you back from achieving other long-term goals. Paying off your debt gives you the room to start saving or investing. Once your debt is under control, you can start thinking about bigger goals, like saving for a home or retirement.

On the other hand, if you are out of debt, you might want to focus on saving for an emergency fund. An emergency fund is one of the most important things you can have. If something unexpected happens, such as a job loss or a medical emergency, having savings available gives you peace of mind and prevents you from going into debt.

Generally, it's a good idea to have three to six months of your monthly expenses saved in a separate, easily accessible account.

Once you have these priorities clear, it's helpful to break your goals down into smaller, attainable objectives. This makes each goal seem less scary and more manageable. If your goal is to save $10,000 in a year, break it down into monthly goals. You'd need to save about $833 each month. And if you break it down even further, that's roughly $28 a day in savings. What small changes can you make in your daily life to save that amount? Maybe stop buying coffee out or cut back on dining out. By breaking down big goals into small daily or monthly actions, it becomes much easier to work toward them.

Another important aspect of prioritization is adjusting your goals based on your resources and situation. As you progress, your priorities may change. Maybe one moment your priority is paying off debt, but later it may be saving for a trip or a personal project. Make sure you regularly review your goals and assess whether they are still aligned with your life. If you have a change of direction or a new opportunity, don't hesitate to adjust your priorities. Life is dynamic, and your goals should be too.

Sometimes people get frustrated because the goals they set seem too big or unattainable. The key is patience and long-term commitment. You may not see results right away, but that doesn't mean you're not making progress. Every step you take, no matter how small, brings you closer to your goal. Consistency is what makes the difference.

Also, never underestimate the power of celebrating your small achievements. Every time you reach one of your smaller goals, celebrate the success. Not only does this give you a sense of accomplishment, but it also reinforces your commitment to keep going. If you've saved up a portion of your goal, take a moment to enjoy what you've accomplished. This type of positive motivation will keep you focused on your goals and help you overcome any obstacles that may arise along the way.

In short, defining your financial goals and prioritizing them is a crucial step to success. When you have a clear plan, you can make decisions with confidence and make sure your money is working for you. It's not about doing everything at once or trying to achieve all of your goals at once. It's about taking small steps, being consistent, and adjusting course as needed. Most importantly, remember that you're motivated by those goals that resonate with you personally. If you focus on what you truly want, the path to financial independence will be much clearer and more attainable.

Your First Crucial Goal

When you're entering the world of personal finance, it's easy to feel overwhelmed by all there is to do. There are so many things you could improve, so many goals you could achieve, that not knowing where to start can be a huge obstacle. The key is to identify your first crucial goal. This goal should be the starting point, the first stepping stone that allows you to build a path to financial stability. It's not about a grandiose or distant objective, but something concrete and attainable that will give you the necessary momentum to keep moving forward.

Once you have defined your financial goals and prioritized what is most important to you, it is time to decide what the first goal you will tackle will be. This goal should be something you can achieve in a relatively short time, something that gives you visible results and allows you to experience success. This does not mean that it should be something trivial or of little importance, but something that gives you confidence that, with effort, you can achieve what you set out to do. If your first goal is too big or difficult to achieve, you may feel frustrated before you even start. Ideally, it should be a realistic challenge that motivates you to keep going.

One of the most common first goals for many people is to build an emergency fund. This fund is crucial because it provides you with a safety net in case of unexpected events. Life is unpredictable, and unexpected expenses such as an illness, a car repair, or a job loss can pop up at any time. Without an emergency fund, these unexpected events can destabilize your finances and cause you to go into debt. An emergency fund is one of the first goals you should achieve because it gives you the stability needed to continue working on your other goals without the constant fear of something going wrong.

An emergency fund should be one of your first goals because when you have one, you can focus on other areas without worrying about unexpected problems. The ideal amount for an emergency fund varies depending on each person's situation, but a general rule of thumb is to save between three and six months of your expenses. This will ensure that you can handle a crisis without having to rely on credit cards or loans. If your monthly expenses are $1,500, an adequate emergency fund would be between $4,500 and $9,000. It may seem like a large amount at first, but the important thing is that you don't have to do it all at once. Start with small savings and gradually increase the amount.

Once you've established your emergency fund, you'll feel much more confident in your ability to handle any crisis. This security is what will give you the motivation to continue to achieve other financial goals. Once you have that foundation, you can start thinking about other long-term goals, such as saving for a home or for your retirement. However, it's important that you don't rush into jumping from one goal to the next. The emergency fund is a critical step that prepares you for any surprises along the way.

When setting your first crucial goal, it's also important to consider how you're going to achieve it. It's not enough to just tell yourself, "I want to save $5,000 in six months" and expect it to happen. You need a concrete plan. To save, for example, you can start by adjusting your monthly expenses and find areas where you can cut back. Look at your recurring expenses and analyze where you're overspending. Maybe you can cut back on the money you spend on eating out, entertainment, or impulse purchases. If you can make these small adjustments, the money you save each month can go straight into your emergency fund.

Additionally, a great way to ensure that you're consistently saving is to automate the process. If you have a portion of your salary automatically transferred into a savings account each month, you won't even have to think about it. The money will be set aside without you having to do anything, making the process much easier and more sustainable. This type of automation allows you to be consistent without having to scramble every month to save.

The key to achieving this first goal is perseverance. There may be months when you feel like you're not progressing as fast as you'd like, or that unexpected events make it difficult to save. At those times, the important thing is not to give up.

Remember that the goal is not perfect, but progressive. Each time you save a little more, you'll be closer to your goal, and the process will teach you the discipline you need to achieve other financial achievements.

If you don't have an extra source of income or your expenses are very tight, don't worry, because there are still ways to reach your goal. You can look for ways to generate additional income, such as selling things you no longer need or doing odd jobs. You can also improve your skills and find ways to increase your value in the job market. Sometimes, even a small amount of extra income can make a big difference in your ability to save and reach your goals.

Remember that achieving your first crucial goal is not just measured in terms of money, but in the progress you have made in the way you think and act regarding your finances. When you reach that first goal, you are not only achieving a specific objective, but you are developing a mindset that will help you achieve everything else you set out to do. You are learning to be responsible with your money, to make conscious decisions, and to prioritize what really matters.

In short, your first milestone goal is a critical step on your path to financial freedom. No matter how big or small it is, the important thing is that it is achievable and motivates you to keep going. Don't underestimate the power of this first step. Over time, achieving this goal will give you the confidence and security needed to tackle other, larger financial goals. Each goal you achieve will be a stepping stone to a more stable and fulfilling financial life. The key is to get started, and that is the real key to transforming your future.

Save For Your Dreams

Saving for your dreams may sound like a motivational phrase, but it's actually one of the most powerful steps you can take to ensure your life aligns with what you truly want. We all have dreams, from buying a home, traveling the world, starting your own business, or even retiring early. However, those dreams don't magically come true. They require planning, effort, and most importantly, saving strategically.

The first step to saving for your dreams is to get clear about what you really want. It's not enough to say "I want to be rich" or "I want to own a house." It's important to be specific. What kind of house do you want? Where? What does "being rich" mean to you? When you clearly define what you want to achieve, it becomes much easier to identify how much money you need to achieve it and how long it will take you to get there. If your dream is to travel the world, how much would that trip cost? For how many months? What places would you like to visit? When your goals are concrete, you can start planning how to make them a reality.

Once you're clear on what you want, the next step is to quantify that dream. It's easy to think in vague terms like "I want to save up for travel," but if you don't know how much you need to save, it's hard to measure your progress. Imagine you want to travel to Europe next year. Research how much the trip would cost, including airfare, lodging, food, and activities. If you estimate the trip will cost $3,000, then you already know how much you need to save. If you'd rather save for a larger project, like buying a home, you can also research average prices in the area where you'd like to live. By knowing the exact amount you need, you can divide that amount by the months or years you have available to save, and that will give you a more attainable goal.

Now that you know what you want and how much you need to save, it's time to make a plan. Saving for your dreams isn't just a matter of putting money in an account and hoping it grows. You need to be disciplined and strategic. One of the most effective ways to do this is to set aside a portion of your income each month exclusively for your dream. Ideally, this amount should be a priority in your budget. If you save for your dreams at the end of the month, when you've already spent on everything else, there probably won't be much money left. Instead, if you make your dream a priority from the start, it will be easier to accomplish. Setting up a separate account just for your dreams also helps prevent you from using that money for other things. When you see the progress of your savings, you're even more motivated to keep going.

At the same time, it's important to be realistic about your ability to save. Don't set goals that are unattainable. If after calculating what you need for your dream you realize that saving that amount in a short time is impossible, then adjust your plan. Perhaps you can extend the time frame for achieving your dream or find ways to increase your income. You might consider selling things you no longer need, offering your services in your spare time, or improving your skills to access better job opportunities. Sometimes saving for a dream requires a little creativity, but it's totally possible if you put your mind to it.

The key is consistency. Saving for your dreams is a process that doesn't happen overnight, but every step you take brings you a little closer to the future you want. Every month you save a little more, every small adjustment in your spending, it all counts. Progress is more important than speed. As you go, you can also learn to be more efficient with your resources. You may not know how to achieve optimal savings at first, but over time, you'll learn to manage your money more wisely, and that will bring you closer to your dreams, too.

One of the most powerful things you can do to stay motivated is to visualize your dream. Imagine how it would feel to have that house you've always wanted, or to be standing in front of the Eiffel Tower after months of planning. Every time you save, think back to that moment. Visualization connects you to your goal and makes the process of saving more rewarding. You can also create a dream board, where you put pictures of what you want to achieve. Seeing those images every day will remind you why you're saving and keep you focused.

Throughout this process, it's important not to get discouraged if you face difficulties. It's normal to have ups and downs on the road to your dreams. There may be months when you don't manage to save as much as you'd like, or unexpected situations that make you deviate from your plan. However, the key is not to give up. If you ever find yourself unable to meet your savings goal, simply adjust the time frame or the amount you save. The important thing is to keep going.

When it comes to your relationship with money, it's important to learn to enjoy the process. Saving for your dreams shouldn't feel like a punishment or a restriction. Instead of seeing it as a loss, think of it as an investment in your future. Every time you make a conscious decision to save for your dream, you're one step closer to achieving something you truly want. This positive mindset is key to staying motivated in the long run.

Finally, once you have reached your goal, the feeling of satisfaction will be incomparable. You will have transformed a dream that seemed far away into a reality.

Not only will you have managed to save the necessary amount, but you will have also acquired a valuable skill: the ability to make your dreams a reality through discipline and effort. This achievement is not only a step towards a specific goal, but a reminder that anything you want really is possible if you are persistent and strategic enough.

In short, saving for your dreams is a process of planning, sacrifice, and perseverance. No matter how big or small your dream is, the important thing is that you take control of your finances and start working towards it. With a clear plan, the right motivation, and a consistent focus, any dream can be achieved. Don't underestimate the power of saving for what you truly want, because every step you take will bring you closer to a life that is aligned with your true desires and goals.

Earn More To Save More

Saving money isn't always just about cutting expenses. While reducing your unnecessary expenses is a powerful strategy, there comes a point when you simply can't cut any more without compromising your quality of life. This is where the other side of the financial equation comes into play: increasing your income. Earning more money not only allows you to save more, but it also gives you greater freedom to reach your goals faster and with fewer sacrifices. It's a powerful tool that we often overlook because it seems more difficult than simply tightening our belts.

The first step to earning more is accepting that your current income doesn't have to be permanent. Many people fall into the trap of thinking that their salary is some sort of fixed limit that can't be exceeded. However, the reality is that there are many ways to increase your income, whether it's within your current job, exploring new career opportunities, or even starting something on your own. The important thing is to change your mindset and start seeing your income as something that is within your control.

One of the most direct ways to earn more money is to seek an upgrade at your current job. If you are employed, consider whether you are maximizing your potential within your position. Have you considered asking for a raise? Often, simply having a conversation with your boss about your performance and your contribution to the company can result in a pay increase. Of course, this requires preparation. Before you ask for a raise, research what the average salary is for your position in your industry and be prepared to make the case for why you deserve to earn more. Talk about the results you have generated, the responsibilities you have taken on, and how you have contributed to the company's success. If you do so in a professional manner, you are likely to get a positive response.

Another option within your current job is to seek promotions or new roles that will allow you to earn more. Often, staying in the same position for too long limits your ability to grow. Talk to your supervisors about career development opportunities and show your willingness to take on new challenges. If your company doesn't offer growth opportunities, consider looking elsewhere. Changing jobs can be one of the quickest ways to significantly increase your income, especially if you have valuable skills that are in high demand.

If it's not possible to earn more within your current job or if you'd rather diversify your income streams, consider generating additional income. Today, there are many options for creating a secondary source of income that you can manage in your spare time. For example, you could offer freelance services in areas where you have expertise, from graphic design and writing to programming or consulting. Platforms like Upwork, Fiverr, and others allow you to connect with clients looking for your specific skills. Even if you don't earn much at first, over time you could build up a portfolio of clients that bring you regular income.

If you don't have specific skills that you can offer as a service, that doesn't mean you can't earn more. There are plenty of other ways to make extra income. You can sell things you no longer need around your home, such as clothes, furniture, or electronics, on platforms like eBay or Facebook Marketplace. You could also learn new skills through online courses and use them to start something new. For example, learning about photography, video editing, or social media can open doors to opportunities you hadn't considered before.

Entrepreneurship is also a powerful way to increase your income. While not all businesses have to start out big, many can be started as small projects that bring in extra money while you keep your main job. For example, you could start a business selling handmade goods, teaching classes in areas where you have expertise, or even creating social media content if you have a particular talent or interest. The important thing is to identify something that you enjoy doing and that is also in demand in the market.

In addition to looking for ways to earn more, it's also crucial that you use that extra money wisely. If you manage to increase your income, avoid the temptation to spend more just because you can. This is known as lifestyle inflation, and it's a silent enemy of your financial goals. Instead of using that money for unnecessary expenses, put it directly toward your savings or goals. For example, if you manage to earn an extra $500 a month and use it to increase your savings, you'll be moving much faster toward your goals.

Focusing on earning more not only has financial benefits, but also personal ones. As you strive to increase your income, you are also developing valuable skills, building a wider network of contacts, and improving your ability to adapt to new situations. All of this has a positive impact on your life in the long run. Earning more is not just about having more money, but about opening doors to new opportunities and experiences that can enrich your life in ways you hadn't imagined.

It's important to note that earning more doesn't always mean working more hours. Often, it's about working smarter, not harder. For example, if you invest time into developing a highly valued skill, you could charge more per hour and work less, but earn the same or even more. This type of strategic approach allows you to balance your income with your time, ensuring that you don't sacrifice your quality of life in the process.

Finally, remember that increasing your income is not a goal you have to achieve overnight. It is a process that requires time, effort, and in many cases, getting out of your comfort zone. But every step you take to earn more brings you closer to your financial goals and the life you want. With an open mindset, a strategic approach, and a willingness to seize opportunities, you can achieve much more than you imagine.

Increasing your income is a powerful tool to transform your financial life. Don't be afraid to explore new possibilities, learn new things, and make the most of your potential. In the end, every effort you make to earn more will not only allow you to save more, but will also give you the confidence and security that you can build a solid financial future full of possibilities.

Stepped Savings

Saving in stages is a strategy that can transform the way you build your finances. Many people feel overwhelmed by the idea of saving large amounts of money right off the bat, and that's completely understandable. If you try to go from saving zero to a significant percentage of your income overnight, you're likely to get frustrated and give up on your plan. This is where saving in stages comes in. This technique allows you to start small and build up your savings gradually, without feeling like you're sacrificing everything all at once.

The core idea of step-by-step savings is simple: you start with a small amount, something that doesn't really bother you. This initial amount can be as low as 1 percent of your income or a fixed amount, like five or ten dollars a week. The important thing isn't how much you save at the beginning, but rather that you get started. This initial amount serves as an easy, manageable step to begin building the habit of saving.

Once you get into the habit of saving that amount, the next step is to gradually increase the amount. For example, you might decide that every three months you'll increase your savings percentage by one percentage point. If you started out saving 1 percent of your income, by the end of the year you'll be saving 4 percent. This gradual approach makes the process much smoother because the increase is so small that you'll barely notice it in your monthly budget.

Saving in stages is especially helpful if your income is limited or you're used to spending most of what you earn. Imagine you're starting from scratch and saving 10 or 20 percent of your income sounds completely out of reach. Instead of getting discouraged, saving in stages allows you to work toward that goal in a progressive manner. Best of all, this method not only helps you save more over time, but it also teaches you to be more mindful of how you use your money.

Plus, this approach has a positive psychological impact. Every time you increase the amount you save, you feel an accomplishment. It's like climbing steps toward a bigger goal. This sense of progress motivates you to keep going and helps you maintain the habit in the long run. Every step you take strengthens your confidence in your ability to manage your finances.

A key aspect of gradual savings is to automate the process as much as possible. If you have to remember to save every month, you're more likely to forget or find an excuse not to. Set up automatic transfers from your main account to a separate savings account. Not only does this ensure that you save consistently, but it also reduces the temptation to spend that money. Once saving becomes automatic, it becomes a part of your life without you having to think about it too much.

Saving in stages is also flexible, making it suitable for any financial situation. If at some point your income increases, you can use that opportunity to scale up your savings faster. For example, if you receive a bonus or a pay raise, instead of spending all of that money, put a significant portion of it toward savings. This way, you adjust the scale upward and speed up your progress. On the other hand, if you face a financial emergency and need to temporarily reduce your savings, you can do so without feeling like you've failed at your goal. Flexibility is one of the great advantages of this method.

This approach also allows you to align your financial goals with your ability to save. You can have short-term goals, like saving for a vacation or an emergency fund, and long-term goals, like a down payment on a house or retirement. Laddered savings helps you work on both at the same time. By progressively increasing the amount you save, you can allocate specific percentages to different goals without feeling like you're overextending yourself.

Another advantage of gradual savings is that it fits well into any stage of life. If you're young and just starting out in your career, you may not be able to save much at first. But with this method, you can start small and increase your contributions as you gain more experience and your income grows. If you're at a later stage in life and haven't saved as much as you'd like, gradual savings allows you to start closing the gap without feeling like you're giving up everything all at once.

The key to success with step-by-step savings is consistency. No matter how small the steps you take, the important thing is to keep moving forward. If you ever feel like progress is slow, remember that every dollar you save is one step closer to your goals. Sometimes the results aren't seen right away, but over time, the accumulation of small savings can be amazing.

A practical example of how phased savings can work is to imagine that you start by saving just five dollars a week. This may seem insignificant, but in one year that's $260. You then decide to increase that amount by five dollars every six months. After the first year, you'll be saving ten dollars a week, and by the end of the second year you'll have accumulated over $780. This example shows how a small start can lead to significant results over time.

Saving in stages also teaches you the importance of patience and long-term planning. Often, we want immediate results, but personal finance doesn't work that way. True progress comes with consistency and discipline, and saving in stages gives you a structure that makes both of those things easier.

In short, step-by-step savings is a powerful tool that allows you to build a solid savings habit without feeling overwhelmed. It helps you start small, increase your savings capacity gradually, and stay motivated with each step you take. In the end, this method not only improves your finances, but it also gives you the peace of mind that comes from knowing that you are moving towards a more secure future full of possibilities. If you have ever felt intimidated by the idea of saving, step-by-step savings is the perfect way to get started. You just need to take the first step and commit to keep taking it one step at a time.

Smart Investments To Grow Your Money

Investing your money is like planting a tree. At first, it doesn't seem like much is happening. You have to tend the soil, water the seeds, and wait patiently. But over time, that little tree grows, bears fruit, and if you take good care of it, can sustain you for years. Investing works in a similar way: it may seem complicated or time-consuming at first, but it's one of the most effective ways to make your money work for you and grow over time.

Many people think that investing is something reserved for financial experts or the wealthy, but this is not true. Today, thanks to technology and the accessibility of markets, virtually anyone can start investing, even with small amounts. The important thing is to have a clear strategy, understand the risks, and start as soon as possible. The longer you let your investments grow, the greater the returns.

The first step to investing wisely is to understand your goals. What do you want to achieve with your investments? It could be saving for your children's education, buying a house, retiring comfortably, or simply generating extra income. Having a clear purpose will help you define how much money you need to invest and what type of investments are best for you. Investing for a short-term goal, such as a vacation, is not the same as investing for a long-term goal, such as retirement.

Once you have your goals clear, it's essential to learn about the different types of investments available. There are many options, and each has its own characteristics, risks, and benefits. For example, investing in stocks means buying a small part of a company. If the company does well, the value of your shares may increase, but if it does poorly, you may also lose money. Stocks are a popular choice for those willing to take on more risk in exchange for higher potential long-term gains.

On the other hand, bonds are a safer investment. When you buy a bond, you're basically lending money to a company or government, and they pay you interest in return. Although the yields are usually lower than stocks, bonds are ideal if you're looking for stability or need a steady stream of income. There are also mutual funds, which are like baskets that group together different assets, such as stocks, bonds, or real estate. Funds are a great option to diversify your investment, which means you reduce risk by not putting "all your eggs in one basket."

Then there are real estate investments, which involve buying properties to rent out or sell at a higher price in the future. This type of investment requires more initial capital, but can be very profitable in the long run. You can also consider real estate investment trusts, which allow you to invest in real estate without having to buy a physical property.

A key aspect of smart investing is understanding the concept of risk and reward. In simple terms, the greater the profit potential of an investment, the greater the associated risk. That's why it's important to know your risk tolerance — how much you're willing to risk without losing your peace of mind. If you're more conservative, you might prefer lower-risk investments like bonds. If you're willing to take on more risk for higher returns, you might consider stocks or cryptocurrencies, although the latter are highly volatile and require a good deal of knowledge before entering.

Diversification is another essential strategy for smart investing. Imagine you're on a boat and suddenly a storm hits. If you have all your weight on one side of the boat, it's more likely to capsize. The same goes for investments. Don't put all your money into one type of asset or one company. Diversifying means spreading your money across different types of investments, industries, and even countries. This way, if one investment doesn't do well, the others can make up for the losses.

For beginners, one of the best ways to get started is by investing through index funds, or ETFs. These are funds that track the performance of a market index, such as the S&P 500. They are easy to understand, have low costs, and offer automatic diversification. Plus, they have a solid track record of generating good returns over the long term. If you don't know where to start, index funds are a great option.

Another important tip is to invest on a regular basis, regardless of what is happening in the market. This is known as periodic investing, and it helps you avoid the mistake of trying to "guess" when the best time to invest is. By investing a set amount of money each month, you buy more when prices are low and less when prices are high. Over the long term, this can lower the average cost of your investments and help you build wealth more consistently.

It's crucial to remember that investing is not a get-rich-quick scheme. In fact, any investment opportunity that promises quick, guaranteed profits is probably a scam. Smart investing requires patience, discipline, and a long-term perspective. Don't worry if the results aren't immediate. The important thing is to stick to the plan and trust the process.

Before you invest, it's also crucial to educate yourself. There are plenty of resources available, from books and blogs to videos and online courses. Learning the basics will give you the confidence to make informed decisions. Also, consider consulting with a financial advisor, especially if you plan to invest large amounts of money or are unsure of where to start. A good advisor can help you develop a customized plan that fits your goals and financial situation.

Finally, make sure to monitor your investments from time to time, but don't get hung up on the market's daily ups and downs. The market is volatile in the short term, but it tends to grow in the long term. Review your portfolio at least once a year to make sure it's aligned with your goals and make adjustments if necessary.

Investing is one of the best ways to grow your money and achieve your financial goals. It doesn't matter if you start small. The important thing is to get started, be consistent, and keep a long-term vision. Over time, your investments can become a source of stability and opportunity, giving you the freedom to live the life you want. Remember, the best time to start investing was yesterday, but the second best time is today. Do it, learn along the way, and let your money work for you.

Optimize your Fixed Expenses and Renegotiate your Contracts

When it comes to saving money, many people first think of cutting small expenses, like stopping buying coffee or limiting eating out. While these actions can add up, there's one source of savings that often goes unnoticed: your fixed expenses. Fixed expenses are those recurring payments you make each month, such as rent, utilities, internet, insurance, and more. The good news is that optimizing these expenses can make a much bigger impact on your finances, and the best part is that this type of savings is permanent. Once you reduce a fixed expense, that reduction is reflected in your budget every month, without you having to make any additional effort.

The first step to optimizing your fixed expenses is to get clear on what they are. Make a detailed list of all the regular payments you make. Include the exact amount, the date you pay, and the service provider. This may seem like a simple task, but you'd be surprised how many people don't know exactly how much they're paying for certain services or even if they're paying for things they no longer use. Once you have this list, you can start analyzing each expense and look for ways to reduce it.

The second step is to identify which of these expenses you can renegotiate. Many services, such as internet, cable, insurance, and even some subscription services, have bargaining margins. Companies don't tell you this outright, but they are willing to offer discounts or better plans if they think you might go with a competitor. This is where strategy comes in. Call them and let them know you're considering switching providers because you found a better deal. Often, just mentioning this will get you a discount to keep you as a customer. If they don't, don't be afraid to shop around. The market is full of competitive options, and in many cases, switching providers can save you a considerable amount.

For insurance, whether it's auto, home or health, shop around at least once a year. Many people stay with the same company for years simply out of convenience, but this loyalty doesn't always translate into better prices. Use online tools to get quotes from multiple companies, and be sure to compare both price and coverage. If you find a better deal, don't hesitate to switch or ask your current company to match the price.

Another major fixed expense worth paying attention to is your rent or mortgage. If you're renting, consider renegotiating your lease when it's due. Research average prices in your area and use that information as a basis for negotiation. Many landlords would rather keep a reliable tenant than have to find a new one, so you might be able to get a rent reduction or some extra perk, such as improvements to the property or a free month. If you have a mortgage, see if you can refinance it to a lower interest rate. This could significantly reduce your monthly payment, though you should carefully evaluate the costs associated with refinancing to make sure it's a good decision.

Besides renegotiating, there are other ways to optimize your fixed expenses. Review your monthly subscriptions. We often subscribe to services like gyms, streaming platforms, or apps that we stop using over time. Analyze whether you are actually using each service and cancel any that are not essential. Even if it seems like a small saving, like ten or fifteen dollars a month, those amounts add up over time.

For utilities like electricity and water, there are many ways to reduce consumption and therefore costs. Switch to energy-efficient light bulbs, unplug electronics you're not using, and consider installing water-efficient showers or toilets. It's also helpful to check if there are energy efficiency programs in your area that can help you reduce these expenses. While it may require a small initial investment, the long-term benefits can be significant.

Don't forget transportation, another major fixed expense in many budgets. If you own a car, consider whether you can cut costs on gas, maintenance, or even car payments. Maybe you can carpool with someone, use public transportation more often, or consider upgrading to a more fuel-efficient vehicle if your current one is a gas guzzler. If you work from home, ask yourself if you really need a car or if you can sell it and save on insurance, gas, and maintenance.

One of the keys to optimizing your fixed expenses is to be proactive. Don't wait for companies to offer you discounts or promotions; look for them yourself. Make it a habit to review your contracts and payments at least once a year. Not only does this help you stay on top of costs, but it also gives you the opportunity to adjust your services to your current needs. For example, if you signed up for a very fast internet plan because you used to work from home, but now you don't need it, you could change to a cheaper plan.

Another important aspect is to keep track of your savings. Every time you manage to reduce a fixed expense, write it down and allocate that extra money to a savings fund or to your financial goals. Not only will this help you stay on top of your finances, but it will also motivate you to keep looking for more savings opportunities. Seeing the cumulative impact of these small changes can be very rewarding.

Finally, remember that optimizing your fixed expenses doesn't mean sacrificing your quality of life. The goal isn't to live on the bare minimum, but to make sure you're paying just enough for the services you really need and use. Sometimes, companies take advantage of our inertia and we continue to pay more than necessary simply because we don't take the time to review our options. By being proactive and aware, you'll not only save money, but you'll also gain peace of mind knowing you're doing what's best for your finances.

Optimizing your fixed expenses and renegotiating your contracts is one of the most effective ways to free up money in your budget. It may take some time and effort up front, but the long-term benefits make it worth it. Don't underestimate the power of small changes to your recurring payments, because those accumulated savings can make a big difference on your path to financial freedom.

The Impact of Financial Minimalism on Your Savings

Financial minimalism is a philosophy that not only transforms your relationship with money, but also simplifies your life in general. It involves focusing on what you truly need and value, eliminating excess and reducing financial distractions. It's not about depriving yourself of everything or living with the bare minimum, but rather finding a balance that allows you to spend on what's truly important to you, while reducing or eliminating unnecessary expenses.

The impact of financial minimalism on your savings is profound because it forces you to question every single expense. In a world where advertising constantly bombards us with messages urging us to buy more and more, adopting this mindset may seem radical, but it can also be the key to achieving financial freedom. When you practice financial minimalism, every spending decision becomes an opportunity to reflect on your priorities and make sure you are aligned with your goals.

A clear example of how financial minimalism works is with your material belongings. We often accumulate things that we don't use, that don't make us happy, and that ultimately just take up space. Every item we buy not only represents an initial expense, but also an ongoing cost in terms of maintenance, storage, and in some cases, mental stress. By taking a minimalist approach, you cut down on these impulse purchases and focus on acquiring only what you truly need and use. Not only does this save you money, but it also helps you value what you already have more.

Financial minimalism also has a direct impact on your recurring expenses. For example, instead of subscribing to several streaming services that you barely use, you could choose one or two that you really enjoy. If you're paying for a gym membership that you never go to, you might consider canceling it and opting for free activities like running outdoors or working out at home. Each such decision frees up money that you can redirect toward your savings or financial goals.

One area where financial minimalism especially shines is in emotional shopping. We've all had days when we're tempted to buy something to treat ourselves or relieve stress. However, these purchases rarely bring us lasting satisfaction. Financial minimalism teaches you to identify these impulses and find more meaningful ways to meet those emotional needs. Maybe instead of spending money on new clothes you don't need, you'd rather invest your time in an activity that truly makes you happy, like reading, meditating, or spending time with friends and family.

Another powerful aspect of financial minimalism is that it helps you free yourself from the pressure of comparison. Instead of measuring your success based on what others own, you focus on what really matters to you. This gives you the freedom to say no to things you don't need, even if they seem like must-haves to others. For example, maybe you don't need the latest phone model if the one you have works perfectly. Not only does this mindset shift allow you to save money, it also reduces the stress and anxiety associated with trying to keep up with societal expectations.

Financial minimalism also fosters a greater awareness of the value of your time. Every time you spend money on something unnecessary, you're actually spending the time it took you to earn that money. By taking a minimalist approach, you become more aware of this trade-off and begin to prioritize expenses that actually improve your quality of life. Instead of working overtime to pay for a new car you don't need, you could opt for a more economical model and use that extra time for activities you're passionate about.

One of the great benefits of financial minimalism is that it not only improves your financial situation, but it also has a positive impact on your mental well-being. When you eliminate financial and material clutter from your life, you feel calmer and more in control. You are no longer trapped in the cycle of working to spend and spending to feel better. Instead, you can focus on building a life that truly fulfills you.

To begin adopting financial minimalism, you can follow a few practical steps. First, review your expenses from the past few months and classify them into two categories: necessary and optional. This will help you identify spending patterns and areas where you can cut back. Then, set clear rules for your future purchases. For example, you could commit to waiting 48 hours before making any non-essential purchases. This gives you time to reflect and decide whether you really need what you are considering buying.

It's also helpful to define your priorities and long-term goals. What do you really want to achieve with your money? Maybe you dream of traveling, buying a house, or just having the peace of mind of knowing that you're prepared for any unexpected events. Having these goals clearly in mind will help you stay focused and avoid unnecessary spending.

Remember that financial minimalism isn't a one-size-fits-all solution. Every person has different priorities and needs, so it's important to tailor this approach to your own life. It's not about giving up everything, but about making conscious choices that reflect your values and goals.

Ultimately, financial minimalism transforms the way you view money and consumption. It frees you from the endless cycle of spending to fill emotional or social voids and allows you to focus on what really matters. Not only will this shift in perspective help you save more, it will also give you a greater sense of purpose and control over your life.

By embracing financial minimalism, you'll find that you can live with less and be happier at the same time. You'll realize that you don't need so much stuff to feel fulfilled, and that by freeing up space in your life, you're also freeing up space in your mind to focus on what really matters. And, as an added benefit, you'll see your savings account grow month after month, giving you the security and freedom you've always wanted.

Budget for Enjoyment

Many people think that budgeting means restricting their spending to the maximum, living with the minimum possible and giving up the small pleasures that make life more enjoyable. However, this perception is far from reality. A good budget is not only a tool to control your finances, but also a way to enjoy your money without feeling guilty. Budgeting for enjoyment is a way to ensure that you are using your money in a way that reflects your values and brings you happiness, while staying on track towards your financial goals.

The most common mistake when budgeting is thinking that every penny should go toward paying off debt or saving, leaving little or nothing for personal enjoyment. This approach can be unsustainable and frustrating, often leading to abandoning the budget altogether. The key is finding a balance that allows you to move forward financially without sacrificing the moments that make you feel fulfilled. This is where the concept of including enjoyment in your budget comes into play.

The first step to budgeting for enjoyment is to recognize that it's okay to spend money on things that make you happy. There's no need to feel guilty about wanting to go out to dinner with friends, buy a book that excites you, or treat yourself every now and then. The important thing is that these expenses are planned and conscious, rather than impulsive. When you allocate a specific portion of your budget for enjoyment, you eliminate the feeling of doing something wrong and can fully enjoy those experiences or purchases.

To start, identify what activities, products, or experiences truly bring you joy. Maybe you love going to the movies, enjoying a good cup of coffee at your favorite coffee shop, or traveling on the weekends. Everyone has different priorities, so it's important to define what enjoyment means to you. Once you're clear on what you value most, you can allocate a portion of your monthly budget specifically for those expenses.

A good rule of thumb is to allocate 5-10% of your monthly income to enjoyment. For example, if you make $1,000 a month, you might allocate $50-100 toward activities that make you happy. This amount may seem small, but you'll be surprised how far it can go when you use it mindfully. Plus, knowing you have this money set aside for enjoyment eliminates the need to turn to credit or feel guilty about spending.

Once you've settled on a budget, create a priority list for your leisure budget. If you have several things you'd like to do, but don't have enough money to cover everything, focus on what excites you the most or gives you the most satisfaction. You might want to spend it all on one special experience, like dinner at a restaurant you've always wanted to try, or spread it out over several smaller activities, like trips to the movies and coffee breaks with friends. Whatever you choose, make sure it aligns with your values and preferences.

Another important aspect of budgeting for enjoyment is being flexible. Life is full of unexpected events and opportunities, like a concert by your favorite band or a last-minute trip with friends. If something comes up that you really want to do, it's okay to adjust your budget to take advantage of it, as long as it doesn't affect your main financial goals. The key is to do it consciously and avoid letting it become an excuse to constantly overindulge.

It's also helpful to plan ahead for larger or more expensive activities. If you know you want to go on vacation in six months or attend a special event, you can create an enjoyment fund and save a little each month to cover those expenses. This way, you won't have to sacrifice your savings goals or resort to debt to pay for something you really want.

Enjoyment doesn't always have to involve big spending. There are many ways to find joy in free or low-cost activities. Taking a walk in the park, hosting a game night at home with friends, learning a new recipe, or enjoying an afternoon reading a book are all examples of things that can be equally rewarding. Even if you have a budget allocated for enjoyment, finding pleasure in the little things is also a way to enrich your life without spending too much.

It's important to remember that the goal of a pleasure budget isn't to justify overspending, but to allow you to enjoy your money responsibly. When you include pleasure in your budget, you're taking control of your finances and proving that you can live fully while making progress toward your goals. It's a way to balance discipline with gratification, which makes it easier to stick to a budget in the long run.

Plus, budgeting for enjoyment can improve your emotional and mental well-being. Financial stress is a leading cause of anxiety for many people, and feeling constantly deprived can intensify those feelings. By allowing yourself to enjoy your resources in a controlled manner, you reduce the pressure and give yourself the opportunity to celebrate your financial achievements, no matter how small.

Finally, remember that the enjoyment budget is a personal tool. There is no perfect formula that works for everyone, and it's okay to adjust your approach as your circumstances or priorities change. The important thing is to give yourself permission to enjoy your money and live a life that makes you feel fulfilled, while keeping your finances under control. This is one of the most effective ways to ensure that your relationship with money is healthy and sustainable in the long term.

Travel and Save

Traveling is one of the most enriching experiences you can have in life. Discovering new places, meeting people from different cultures, and creating unforgettable memories are reasons enough for many to dream of traveling the world. However, the cost of travel can be intimidating and make some people view it as an unattainable luxury. The good news is that it is possible to travel without spending a fortune, as long as you adopt smart strategies to save before, during, and after your adventure.

The first step to traveling and saving is planning. A well-planned trip not only reduces stress, but can also save you a significant amount of money. Start by defining your destination and setting a realistic budget. Research how much flights, accommodation, local transportation, food, and activities cost in the place you want to visit. Having a clear idea of costs will help you set a specific savings goal and prioritize your spending.

An effective strategy for saving on travel is to be flexible with dates. Flights and accommodations are often cheaper outside of peak seasons, when there is less demand. If you can travel on weekdays or during less busy months, you can find much cheaper deals. Tools like flight search engines allow you to compare prices on different dates and find the lowest fares.

Also, consider destinations that are easy on your wallet. While some places are famous for being expensive, there are many others that are equally fascinating and affordable. Countries in Asia, Latin America, or Eastern Europe, for example, offer unique experiences at much lower prices than traditional destinations. Researching alternative options can open the door to adventures you never imagined possible.

Once you've decided on your destination and dates, look for budget-friendly options for transportation and accommodation. For flights, use price comparison sites and sign up for alerts to receive notifications of deals or promotions. You can also explore options like low-cost airlines, which often offer reduced fares if you're willing to forgo certain extras, such as choosing your seat or carrying extra luggage. For accommodation, platforms like hostels, vacation rentals, or even home exchanges can be cheaper alternatives to traditional hotels.

Another key to saving money when traveling is cutting back on food and drink. Eating out at restaurants every day can quickly eat into your budget. An alternative is to look for accommodations with kitchens and prepare some of your own meals. Additionally, exploring local markets is not only a fascinating cultural experience, but it also gives you access to fresh, affordable food. If you do choose to eat out, look for recommendations from places frequented by locals, as they are often more authentic and less expensive than tourist sites.

As for activities, many cities offer free or low-cost attractions that can be just as exciting as more expensive options. For example, walking through parks, visiting museums on free admission days, or joining walking tours can give you a unique perspective of the place without breaking the bank. It's also helpful to look into whether destinations offer tourist passes that include access to multiple attractions for one reduced price.

Local transportation is another area where you can save considerably. Instead of relying on taxis or ride-hailing services, use public transportation whenever possible. Many cities have efficient and affordable subway or bus systems that will allow you to get around without breaking the bank. Walking or renting a bike are also great ways to explore and enjoy your destination while keeping costs down.

To fund your travels without breaking the bank, it's important to include them as a specific goal in your budget. Allocate a portion of your monthly income to a travel fund and be disciplined with your savings. Cutting back on small, unnecessary expenses in your daily life, like eating out frequently or subscriptions you don't use, can free up money that you can put toward your next trip.

If traveling is something you're really passionate about, you can also look for ways to generate additional income to fund it. Maybe you can sell things you no longer need, work as a freelancer, or find some temporary work. Every extra dollar you earn brings you closer to your goal and reduces the strain on your main budget.

Once you arrive at your destination, stay on top of your spending. Set a daily budget and try to stick to it. Keeping track of what you spend not only helps you stay on plan, but it also allows you to identify areas where you could adjust and save even more. While it's important to enjoy the moment, maintaining financial discipline while traveling will ensure you don't get an unpleasant surprise when you return home.

Finally, remember that luxury is not synonymous with enjoyment. Some of the most memorable experiences cost nothing or very little. Watching a sunset, chatting with a local, exploring picturesque streets or simply enjoying nature are priceless moments that enrich your travels in ways that money can't buy.

Traveling doesn't have to be a privilege reserved for a select few. With planning, flexibility, and smart decisions, you can make it a regular part of your life without compromising your financial stability. Saving to travel is not only possible, but also a way to prove to yourself that your dreams are achievable when you work for them. Thus, each experience becomes a reminder that effort and dedication are worth it.

The Importance of Rewarding Yourself

Saving and managing your personal finances requires discipline, patience, and often sacrifice. Deciding to postpone a purchase, resisting a temptation, or putting that extra money into your savings fund instead of spending it on something immediately are acts of willpower that aren't always easy. That's why rewarding yourself is a crucial part of the process. Not only is it a way to celebrate your achievements, but it's also a way to keep yourself motivated to continue on the path to your financial goals.

Many people have the misconception that saving means constantly depriving themselves of things they enjoy. However, this mindset can backfire in the long run. If all your efforts to save are accompanied by a feeling of restriction and deprivation, you're likely to feel frustrated or unmotivated at some point. This is where the importance of giving yourself small rewards that recognize your progress and help you enjoy the journey as you continue to build a more secure future comes in.

Rewarding yourself doesn't mean spending a lot of money or sabotaging your financial goals. It's about finding meaningful ways to celebrate your progress, tailored to your budget and personal interests. Maybe you managed to save enough to cover a month's expenses, got out of a major debt, or reached 50% of your savings goal for a vacation. These are accomplishments that deserve to be recognized and celebrated.

The first step to including rewards in your financial plan is to define what a reward means to you. For some, it might be a special outing with friends, a spa day, or dinner at a restaurant they've always wanted to try. For others, it could be something simpler, like buying a book, enjoying an afternoon watching their favorite movie, or taking some time to relax guilt-free. No matter what you choose, the important thing is that it's something that truly makes you feel good and motivates you to keep going.

One way to structure your rewards is to tie them to your financial goals. For example, you might decide that every time you complete a major step in your savings plan, you'll give yourself a reward. If you're working to save three months of emergency expenses, you could plan a small celebration every time you save one of those months. Not only does this system give you something to look forward to, it also makes the process of saving feel more tangible and rewarding.

It's important that rewards are proportional to the achievement. It wouldn't make sense to spend a significant amount of money on a celebration if you're just starting to build your emergency fund or if you're trying to get out of debt. Rewards don't have to be expensive to be effective. For example, you could celebrate with a special night at home, making your favorite meal, watching a movie you're excited about, or simply taking time to enjoy an activity you love.

If you decide that your reward will be something that involves spending, plan ahead and make sure to budget for it. By doing so, you'll avoid feeling guilty about spending money and will be able to fully enjoy the experience. Plus, planning your rewards helps you stay in control of your finances and prevents you from overindulging on emotional impulses.

Rewarding yourself can also be a way to reinforce positive habits. For example, if you managed to stay within your budget for three months in a row, you could give yourself a reward that motivates you to continue that behavior. In this way, you're training your brain to associate responsible financial actions with feelings of satisfaction and happiness.

Also, remember that rewards don't always have to be material. Many times, experiences are more valuable and rewarding than objects. A walk in nature, an afternoon with loved ones, or even a day off to yourself can be very meaningful ways to celebrate your accomplishments. These experiences not only bring you satisfaction, but they also create memories that will stay with you long afterward.

Rewarding yourself not only benefits you emotionally, but it can also improve your relationship with money. When you learn to balance saving with enjoyment, you are developing a healthier and more sustainable financial mindset. You realize that money is not just a tool to pay bills or accumulate in a savings account, but also a means to live a full and meaningful life.

It's important to keep in mind that rewards shouldn't become an excuse to overindulge or justify unnecessary spending. Always keep your main goals in mind and make sure that rewards are aligned with your financial plan. The idea is not to sabotage your progress, but to celebrate it responsibly.

Finally, rewarding yourself is a way to remind yourself how far you've come. Sometimes the road to financial goals can feel slow or even overwhelming, but when you take a moment to acknowledge your progress, it's easier to stay motivated and focused. Every small accomplishment is one step closer to your dreams, and celebrating it gives you the energy you need to keep going.

The key is to find a balance that works for you, one where you can enjoy the present without losing sight of the future. By rewarding yourself, you're not only celebrating your financial achievements, but you're also learning to enjoy your life in a mindful and fulfilling way. And that, at the end of the day, is the true purpose of money: to help you build a life you love while achieving your goals.

From Saver to Mentor

Saving can start out as a personal necessity, an act of responsibility toward yourself and your future. But over time, what you learn during that process has the potential to transcend and benefit others. Becoming a financial mentor is not only a way to share your experience, but also to consolidate your own habits and knowledge. When you teach, you also learn. Helping others take control of their finances can be a deeply rewarding experience, both emotionally and personally.

The first step in moving from saver to mentor is to recognize the value of your experience. You may feel like you don't have enough knowledge or that you're not a financial expert, but that's not true. If you've managed to save consistently, set a budget, get out of debt, or invest your money wisely, you have something valuable to share. The important thing is not to have perfect answers, but rather the willingness to share what has worked for you in an honest and genuine way.

Start by identifying people who could benefit from your guidance. Maybe they are friends, family members, or colleagues who are struggling with their finances. Someone close to you may have commented at some point that they don't know where to start or that they feel overwhelmed by their debt. These are opportunities to offer help in a friendly, non-invasive way. Sometimes all someone needs is a little nudge or some initial guidance to start making better financial decisions.

When talking to someone about their finances, it's crucial to create an environment of trust and support. Talking about money can be a sensitive topic, and many people feel embarrassed or uncomfortable admitting their financial problems. Listen without judgment and show empathy. Share your own financial challenges and how you overcame them. Showing your vulnerability can help the other person feel more comfortable and willing to open up.

A good financial mentor doesn't give orders or impose their vision. Instead of telling someone what to do, they help the person reflect on their situation and come to their own conclusions. You can ask questions like: What are your financial goals? What expenses do you feel you could cut back on? What small steps do you think you could take this week? This approach encourages autonomy and commitment, which are essential to achieving lasting change.

As you share your knowledge, it's also important to tailor your message to the needs and circumstances of the person you're speaking to. Every financial situation is unique, and what worked for you may not be applicable to everyone. For example, if someone has a limited income, they might need a different approach to saving compared to someone who has a higher salary but lots of unnecessary expenses. Actively listen and adjust your advice based on what's most relevant to them.

Being a mentor doesn't mean having all the answers. In some cases, the person you're working with may need additional resources or professional help. For example, if someone is dealing with significant debt or legal issues involving money, you might suggest they consult a financial advisor or a specialized attorney. Being a good mentor involves knowing when to refer someone to an expert and recognizing the limits of your knowledge.

In addition to helping individuals directly, you can also inspire more people through actions and examples. You may want to share your experiences on social media, write a blog about personal finance, or even give talks in your community. These are powerful channels to reach a wider audience and convey your learnings in an accessible way. Remember that every little piece of advice can make a big difference in someone's life.

Mentoring not only benefits the person receiving your advice, but it also strengthens your own financial habits. Talking about your strategies, reflecting on your successes, and learning from the questions others ask you helps you deepen your knowledge. Often, mentoring others forces you to think about your own processes in a more structured way and gives you new ideas for improvement.

One of the greatest rewards of being a financial mentor is seeing the positive impact you can have on the lives of others.

Helping someone get out of debt, build an emergency fund, or simply feel more confident about their finances can be incredibly satisfying. Knowing that you've contributed to someone's more stable and less stressful life is a powerful reminder that your own efforts to learn and improve also serve a greater purpose.

Being a mentor also allows you to convey a broader message about the importance of financial education. Many of the financial problems people face are not the result of bad decisions, but rather a lack of basic knowledge about how to manage money. By sharing what you know, you are helping to close that gap and empower others to take control of their financial situation.

Becoming a mentor doesn't require you to be perfect or have achieved all of your financial goals. It's a process where you grow along with the people you help. As you share what you've learned, you'll also constantly remind yourself why you started your own savings journey and what motivates you to keep going.

Ultimately, being a financial mentor is a way to extend the impact of your personal effort beyond yourself. It's an act of generosity that creates a ripple effect, as the people you help can inspire others to make better financial decisions. So what started as a personal effort to save can become a positive change in your community and beyond.

www.ingramcontent.com/pod-product-compliance
Lightning Source LLC
La Vergne TN
LVHW090419210926
848480LV00002B/628